XX: A Poetic Insight Into Womanhood

CURTIS-ROY WORRALL

Order this book online at www.trafford.com
or email orders@trafford.com

Most Trafford titles are also available at major online book retailers.

Printed in the United States of America.

ISBN: 978-1-4907-0566-8 (sc)
ISBN: 978-1-4907-0565-1 (e)

Trafford rev. 05/14/2014

 www.trafford.com

North America & international
toll-free: 1 888 232 4444 (USA & Canada)
fax: 812 355 4082

Contents

XX

A genetic code of XX makes us unique, as
because of 23 pairs, humans we are.
Five percentage in our cells may be a low number, but
it is double compared to our male counterparts.
One X chromosome is from our mother and the other
X chromosome is from our parental grandmother.
It may be strange that my genetic code comes from
two seperate generations, but that makes me me.
The information that I carry, commonly known as my genes
is significantly a lot, compared with the Y chromosome.
Therefore I am more complexed and
complicated than my male counterpart.
Two thousand genes is a lot on the X chromosome,
compared to 78 genes on the Y chromosome. That
is probably why males seem more simple and basic.
And remember I have two of the X chromosomes.

You can buy me a drink, but you cannot buy my heart

So you want to buy me a drink.
You want to show me your wad of cash.
You think that my heart is for sale.
Even a millionaire could not afford me.

So ply your efforts in order to impress me.
I may act thankful, but do you see the euro signs in my eyes.
You will be poor by the end of the night.
And you will be definately sleeping alone tonight.

Will you learn your lesson and become wisier in your actions?
Or will you give it another try?
We are here to gain respect.
And that is something that money cannot buy!

Models

Look at me, what do you see?
It is never about you, it is all about me.
I am tall and slim, what more do you want?
If I was a letter, I would be a beautiful font.
Chanel, Versace and Armani is all I know.
Check out the label, it us all I need to show.
I am here to parade on the catwalk.
Tell me your opinion, let me hear you talk.
I am the best you can get, so show me respect.
I am so beautiful, I have nothing to regret.
Show me the money, as I have expensive taste.
For me, you should always have money to waste.

The Modern Pandora's Box

The contents are not all the evils of the world.

Nor is it a chamber where a new life can be nurtured.

The contents is knowledge and wisdom about all mankind.

But this chest/box can only be opened with a godlike key.

So the owner of this wonder is not who you think it is.

The Greek gods have no involvement in its possesion.

It is the feminists who decide its role in society.

But the owner must not use this special

facility to their own advantage.

The advantage must be for all the women

that the owner comes into contact with.

Womanhood is becoming a honoured privilege.

And with this object, women will truely

become like Pandora herself.

Motto

Shall we embark on a journey where
two lovers find true paradise?

Lunar Sensitive

I have a cycle governed by the celestral
object which I see almost every night.
I have peaks and ultimate peaks.
I share the connection with tidal waves.
And I have more energy when the moon is full.
In sink, I feel with an omitting energy.
Not a werewolf, but a sensitive creature.
Where I can roam freely and make that special connection.
So see me in the periods, where I succumb
to, and witness a remarkable effect.

The Forbidden Fruit

My desire for you knows no limits.
I lust for you every second of the day.
My body craves you every waking moment.
I am addicted to your alluring taste.

When you are not in my vicinity, I miss your company.
If you are not close, my body yearns for your presence.
My heart beats quicker, when you are nearby.
I am at peace, when you are in my surroundings.

My mouth waters when I taste your flavour.
You compliment my yang with your yin.
Only you can give me that inner peace.
Please stay with me and mature my tendency.

You are unique and one of a kind.
You satsify every tastebud in my being.
Delicious and tasty you definately are.
But I know of no other greater reward.

Female Values

Stand your ground.
Use your voice.
Hear the sound.
It's your choice.

You are strong.
Set a trend.
The path is long.
Make amend.

Feel your power.
In women we trust.
Enjoy the desire.
Life is much more than lust.

We are equal, but not the same!

So now due to society's demands, we are finally equal.
The fight for equality has been definately won.
But now the premise has another twist.
As we are in control, and it is not going to our heads.
With us at the helm, we will go in another direction.
We will be the finest examples.
We know we can do it better than our previous predecessors.
So watch how our future unfolds.
Directness is not always the best policy.
We were always wise in our thought processes.
Intelligent we are and we see the result.
The time has come to accept our targets.
The shift will be gradual, but you will see it's effort.
We forget nothing and we will always remember.
Pioneers and leaders are what we are.
So enjoy the new era with a pleasant buzz.
The power is in our hands and we will not let it squander.
The time is right to follow in our footsteps.
Believe and trust in us, as we are in the driving seat.
Casualities of war will not occur, as we do not need to fight.
We predict a positive and bright outcome, that is for certain.
We have dwelled for too many years.
Consequence is something that we are getting accustomed to.
So enjoy the environment and setting that we have created.

Motto

Women are there to be discovered. Every
contact should be a telling experience.

The Crusade!

I can definately make a diffence.
My will grows tenfold everyday.
I can help all women who need assistance.
And the path I walk upon is known only to me.
So see the development in modern society.
As I will be seen as a character who
is on this planet seldomly.
I will succeed in all that I venture in.
So watch this space and see the alternative.

Compactability

Your desire is my desire.
Your thoughts are my thoughts.
Your actions are my actions.
Your will is my will.

Your favourites are my favourites.
Your senses are my senses.
Your feelings are my feelings.
Your passion is my passion.

Your hope is my hope.
Your emotions are my emotions.
Your joy is my joy.
Your connection is my connection.

Your happiness is my happiness.
Your admiration is my admiration.
Your boundaries are my boundaries.
Your exploration is my exploration.

Your presence is my presence.
Your aim is my aim.
Your response is my response.
Your love is my love.

Motto

In an ideal world, I would sleep with all of you, but
in the real world, I do not sleep with any of you.

I want to be your friend,
not your lover

I want to be your friend, not your lover.
My actions are as I am undercover.
My male counterparts think I should take it a step further.
But that for me would be like mixing beer with cider.

I believe in a plutonic relationship.
Let's not complicate things with love.
Friendship can be such a strong medium.
We belong together as best friends.

I want to be your friend, not your lover.
I am not around you, as if I want to hover.
You can cry on my shoulder if you need to.
I do not get scared when someone goes boohoo.

I believe in a plutonic relationship.
Let's not complicate things with love.
Friendship can be such a strong medium.
We belong together as best friends.

I want to be your friend, not your lover.
I want to be like a sister, not like a mother.
I hope we can find a solution.
And the situation has a higher resolution.

The One That Got Away!

So you are no longer under my limelight.
As the saying goes; out of mind, out of sight.
You are in a stronger position without
my presence and direction.
By the action of my withdrawal, you
are closer to perfection.
I have fond memories of you, that is for sure.
But you have left me alone, by walking out of the door.
You prefer to look forward and not in the past.
You would not be with me, even if I was the last.
So lets celebrate your freedom with a toast.
And I hope you live your life to the most.
No goodbyes are needed as you are gone.
But when you were near, the sun shone.

Women!

The most important thing to do is to respect them.
If you want more, then why not entice them.
Before you know it, you can discover them.
And then it will be effortless to explore them.
If there is a click, why not attract that special one?
Then you can enjoy the art of stimulation.
The contact will be equal and then why
not try to seduce the favourable.
But try not too hard to be indifferent.
So enjoy the greatest challenge with your heart in place.
The thought will be clearly pensive.
So yearn for that other half.
And when you meet that specific one, you can be attentive.
The knowledge of women will be a great feat.
So judge very women by her character.
Soothe her when it is time to respond.
But remember that every woman can be a strong mistress.

The Combustive Concoction Effect!

You are like a wild fire and I am like
an infinite source of oil.
Together we purify our surroundings and
produce a beautiful visual display.
We engulf all problems and burn them to cinders.
We are an inflicting duo and there is
nothing that can stand in our path.
Your passion and my commitment ensures
we will succeed in all that we connect.
We can become the most famous double act in history.
So indulge in my presence and I will heighten your senses.
And we will oxidise the world around us.

The Nut

You seem like a hard nut to crack.
I try my hardest, but you give me no slack.
Even adaption is not enough to get me on the right track.
Will I ever get you in the sack?

Full of energy and hard to break.
Honest and full of truth and never fake.
When I see you, I am wide awake.
Except my advances for goodness sake.

I will never give up on you, as I am fully addicted.
I am also extremely committed.
I do not know the outcome, it is not predicted.
I want to be with you, but it is not promitted.

Motto

I prefer blondes, but the rest are too beautiful to ignore.

Women Rule!

You all had the power.
You all set the direction in the way that you desired.
You all made that telling decision.
You all moulded your world into a form that was beneficial.
But now your power is becoming a luxurious talent.
You have more factors to consider.
You have to realise that there will be
lambs that will be slaughtered.
And you must sever from those, so that
you will not be underminded.
So face your challenges with a new motto.
You need to win this endless war/
Your predecessors were used to the battle.
Now you have to discover that fulfilling emotion.
Feel the power that you always had.
Be strong in your beliefs and never give in.
Before the losers were people that you did not care for.
Now the losers are those that were at
least once close to your heart.

Lipstick & High Heels

Check me out, I have made the effort.
I hope that I stand out in the crowd.
My body may be accentuated and visually strengthened.
So give me the attention that I deserve.

Don't Be A Stranger!

So finally our paths have crossed.

It seems like I waited an eternity for our first meeting.

But now the direction is in our hands.

So lets see how far we can travel together.

What first seemed like a casual encounter.

Has heightened to a phenomenal degree.

I believe in fate, so our next encounter

will be in the near future.

And I anticipate a warm reunion.

The clock may be ticking, but I am not counting.

I know all will fall into place.

The time has come to transmit the signal.

So recieve my transmittion and become the reciever.

Motto

There are no two women that are the same. Everyone is an individual with their own personality and character, so I explore their womenhood with an eagerness that is worth every waking moment.

I Am The Joker

You may mock me and laugh at my expense.
But I will always have the last laugh.
You may ridicule me to higher your status.
But then again, I will jest and keep you beneath me.
And surely you will banter to reinforce your presence.
But in the end, you will be amused by my rendition.
So I wait in anticipation for the applause to happen.
As I am the imfamous jester who is far from being the fool.

Heroines

The most common heroine is usually your mother.
She nurtured you and got you out of bother.
A best friend was there to help you on your way.
She could communicate with you and knew what to say.
A sister was there to assist when it got tough.
She stood by you when the going got rough.
A grandmother's advice was invaluable and crystal clear.
Then admitably you had nothing to fear.
In the historical world, Joan of Arc won the war.
And her status symbol opened the cerebral door.
In the Hollywood scene, Angeline Jolie is a strong icon.
She is a bright star, which as certainly shone.
As for music, Beyonce is up there with the greats.
Her connection with her fans is a wonderful trait.
Mother Theresa was a giver in a moneyless world.
She had great courage and was definately bold.
Princess Diana was an English princess and gave all she got.
Priceless in her actions and was appreciated an invaluable lot.
Rosa Parks sat on the bus and remained seated.
Even when the conversation got heated.
And finally Rosa Luxemburg was a German pioneer.
And helped fellow females on the feminist frontier.

The Flower (Part II)

You are so delicate, I am scared I will break you.
You are so unique, I am worried that you are too precious.
You are so rare, I do not know how to handle you.
You are so fragile, I do not want to damage you.
You are like an antique, I do not want to lose you.
You are so pure, I do not want to tarnish you.
You are so different, I can see no comparison.
You are so beautiful, I am embraced by your presence.
You are so special, I cannot part with you.
You are still growing, I have to let you develop.
When you blossom, you will be the greatest
reward a person can recieve.

Motto

Nothing lasts forever, everything comes in periods.

I am not a magnet!

How can it be that I replicate a magnetic field which
is invisible and it attracts and repels other people. I
have this phenomenal effect since I was born, but I
seem to attract those that interest me for not even a
milisecond, and I repel those that I desire to discover.
I may have iron in my blood, I am not a fatal anemiac, due
to lack of cobalt, and I do not have too much nickel in my
kidneys, bones or thyroid gland, so it is not life threatening.
So I ponder why there is a vector when i meet someone,
and I wish I had more control of the situation.
I have no problem with my bank cards or if
I watch a video or listen to a cassette.
So please do not interact with me if
you feel a magnetic energy.
If you feel it, then I am just smiling and bluffing.

Know Your Competitors/Rivals

There is a trend occuring which affects us all.
The young are changing the interaction with
others and those who are adults are struggling
with the motions which governs their loves.
So beware of those who are now children, for
they dictate how far they can push you.
It is time to break the mould, you are so different
from others, who are older than you, but the
young do not believe in brotherhood of man.
Women must believe in interaction and not resort
to fighting over the ones that they desire.
Men are accustomed to this battle of
egos, but it is new for women.
So embrace your power and defeat those who
wish others that you personally adhere to.
The scars of the battle will be emotional,
so be strong and remain calm.
For now the battle is becoming a battle between
women, and the men are just watching the
efforts of your mercy and joys of war.

You Are The Love Of MY Life!

I have searched high and low to find you in person.
I feel that the search is over, that is for certain.
Now I have to be ambitious and respond to your actions.
I wait in earnest for your loving sanctions.
The path is clear, all we need to do is follow its' direction.
The destination will lead to a true perfection.
The journey will be worth its weight in gold.
Explore with me until we both grow gracefully old.
Who knows what our fruitful future will bring.
We will accept every challenge and will definately win.
So trust in me, and give me a try.
I will love you endlessly till the die I die.
The wait is over and a new chapter has started.
I imploy you to accept my advances fully hearted.
I will not disappoint you and I promise you this.
This is our greatest chance that we should not miss.
I believe that this is meant to be.
Open your eyes and you will see.
The time is right, so accompany me on my mission.
And it will be the greatest transition.

Motto

When at a venue, never approach a woman in the
last hour, as the interaction can be inferred as sexual
interest, but if a woman approaches you, adapt!

It Is Just A Facade!

I should recieve an Oscar for my role in our encounter.
You really do think that I am into you.
I am just a fantastic actress, can't you tell?!
I am definately playing you for a fiddle.
So enjoy the feeling, because it will not last.
Tomorrow you will be analysing where you went wrong.
You pressed my buttons, but got the wrong reaction.
But you will never be on the jury.
So lick your wounds, because you will soon alone.
I am here to find that special one.
The act of acting is my greatest gift.
And believe me, it is far from a facade.

Grab The Baton And Go For Gold!

The race for the imfamous title is about to be concluded.

So show your ability and prove your worth.

Your talent is phenomenal and is obvious to see.

So prove to the world that you are a winner.

The contest is formidable and only the best can succeed.

But thankfully, you certainly fit into that catagory.

Anticapition is always a luxurious hope.

So show your qualities and perform a personal best.

The world will applaud you, as you will

be written in the history books.

And it will be for all the right reasons.

Creme de la creme is what you are.

So enjoy the accolade and compete to your natural best.

I Yield To Your Beauty

I cannot escape from your allure anymore.

I surrender to your temptation.

I cannot resist my actions for now I must act.

Therefore I give up to a superior power.

My motions must be seen as a gesture.

And I see visually someone who is perfect.

I abandon my fear of being rejected.

And banish my perception of myself being mediocre.

I see you as a queen of individual plesentment.

Your features are a wonderous display.

So accept my charms and complete me wholly.

As your presence fulfills my desire to exceptionally

accept the honour of loving you.

Scanners!

I check out the ones I seek.

Eye contact is all we need to start the ball rolling.

I view everything in my environment, and all in its vicinity.

I see many faces per minute.

So if you feel contact is required, then walk in my direction.

And then see what possibilities will occur.

I am here and I will see some action.

So embrace my presence and make me whole.

Flirting Without A Cause

I make eye contact with you to win you over.
And then we have a pleasant conversation.
I place my hand softly on your back.
And we slowly become intimate.
We feel tranquil and the feelings begin to surface.
But we do not become too close.
Kissing is an option, but we choose to be single entities.
And then we swap telephone numbers and
the future seems to pan itself out.
The thought of sex seems never to occur.
But we seem to have a special connection.
I am the master of making you feel like a queen.
And emotional sex with words makes you want more.
So follow my guidance and feel at ease.
As you feel like a woman who is sensually alert.

We Always think
Three Steps Ahead

We think which permutations can occur.
And we hope for an advantagous situation will incur.
Admitably hope plays a big part in our destiny.
And we adjust to all the positive options.
Time is something that we cannot alter.
And so we need to be extremely selective.
As we can lure those close to us to
make that correct decision.
So watch this space and we foresee a positive outcome.

Just The Tonic!

You have a soothing medicinal effect on me.
When you are in my vicinity, I am far from blue.
You take me to a nirvana and the
feeling is tranquil and peaceful.
As your interaction is second to none.
You are a remedy for a lonely heart.
From day one, you emphasised a
willingness to discover more.
So embark on a journey where the destination is true love.
And enjoy the awe in all of its commonities.
You can heal all my aching dilemnas.
And ease the flaws that burden me.
For you have a special gift which I have discovered.
So invigorate my body, soul and mind.

What A Gem!

I have mined and ploughed the world, in
order to discover a gem like you.
Your worth is more than a 1000 carat.
You have a presence which is second to none.
And your value is amplified by your character.
The world wants you to bond with that special one.
And it is marvelous that you chose to be with me.
Your beauty is colossal and I am in awe.
So lets travel together on a journey
where eternity is the destination.

Globalize Me!

You are definately not the girl next door.
I need to jump on a bus, train, ship or plane to see you.
You are far from local, but I do not care.
On route, I see the world when seeing you.
I get to see continents whilst we build a relationship.
I hear many languages, but we speak
in the language of love.
We are city based people, and we get to discover
capital cities such as London, Amsterdam, Cairo,
Pretoria, New Delhi, Tokyo, Bangkok, Mexico City,
Washington D.C, Canberra and Brasilia.
I am never bored as you open up my world.
And I am seduced by your globalized personality.

The Vegetarian Black Widow

Reluctantly I am attracted to your beauty.

Will I make it throught the night?

Your venom could see me waiting at the pearly gates.

But you ensure I live to see another day.

So I live in hope for a restbite.

And I hope that you will freely accept my advances.

I am bemused by your affinity.

And I hope I will not need a paramedic.

So I take a chance to be involved with you.

But you can end my existence.

A promise is a promise, that is clearly stated.

Could it be that you love me so much that

you accept the role of a vegetarian?

The Skeleton Key

I possess a key which can open any type of lock.
It can also lower any barrier, mental or physical.
The key is solely in my possession and it can never be lost.
So watch me open all available doors, and
see that I am completely in control.
With this key, I am able to confront any situation.
I can wield my key and everyone stares in amazement.
No person can understand or grasp how I
can be in such an illustrious position.
I am on this planet to create a possiblity
in which only I can succeed.

The Sublime Gender

Your kind are a supreme being.
I am fascinated by your nature.
Advanced in style and no need for guile.
Greatness emulates from your pores.
Such is the extremitiy of your beauty, I
am phrased by your presence.
But you harness me, and then I have no need for guidance.
The conquest is alluring and I choose
to fight for your pursuit.
As the quest is a long and enduring battle.
The strength in you compels me to also to be so strong.
And the will of mankind will surface in
me, and then we can collaborate.
And the gender complexity will be resolved.

Lightning Source UK Ltd.
Milton Keynes UK
UKOW04f0319120315

247741UK00001B/67/P